A YEAR OF MONEY AND ABUNDANCE

LI-LING OOI

Bailbrook Lane is an imprint of Xelium Ltd.
Published in the United Kingdom
© Li-ling Ooi 2020
The moral rights of the author have been asserted.

First published 2020

All rights reserved. No part of this publication may be reproduced, stored in a retrieval system, or transmitted, in any form, or by any means, without the prior permission in writing of Bailbrook Lane, or as expressly permitted by law, or under terms agreed with the appropriate reprographics rights organisation.

Enquiries concerning reproduction outside the scope of the above should be sent to enquiries@bailbrooklane.com

You must not circulate this book in any other binding or cover and you must impose the same condition on any acquirer.

Ooi, Li-ling

A Year of Money and Abundance/ Li-ling Ooi.

ISBN: 978-1-913557-01-0 (PRINT)

ISBN: 978-1-913557-00-3 (ePUB)

FOREWORD

It has been said that we create for ourselves the things that we need the most.

This is certainly true of the Money Mantras that you are now reading. In creating and writing the mantras we have helped ourselves in more ways that we can even begin to imagine.

The change from simple little statements that have initially felt so bizarrely weird and untrue, now help us revel in our own worthiness and value.

It is our wish for you that each mantra helps you reach for *that* place – that place of understanding, believing and knowing that you are so, so worthy.

Worthy of every good thing, dream, wish and desire that you may be able to imagine and so many more that you may not yet.

HOW TO USE THIS BOOK

Each and every one of us...we are the sum of all our thoughts.

When you realise how much of what you think, defines who you are, you begin to understand that at every moment in time, you have the power to choose – choose what you say, choose how you react, choose what you think.

These mantras were originally written as a weekly guide to help us focus on the wealth, abundance and beauty in the world around us.

They were meant to serve as a grounding point; a place to return to, to remind ourselves that our thoughts and emotions colour all of our perceptions, including and especially those relating to wealth and abundance.

As we began to share the mantras with the world, they came to grow in their reach and their ability to help the people they touched, grow more in to themselves and learn to believe in their own inherent worthiness and goodness.

You may read this book in the order in which the mantras have been arranged or if you wish, simply open it up to any page that you feel called to; either way works.

Each mantra has been written to be focussed upon, one week at a time.

One mantra, one week allows you to focus and eventually placate and internalise the thoughts, messages and emotions that the mantra aims to raise you up to.

That said, do allow yourself to move on, or move forward either through the book or by simply picking another mantra at random to define your week, if the one you are on, simply does not work for you.

There really is no right or wrong way to do this.

There is simply the way that feels best to you and for you.

Trust in your instincts; trust in yourself.

HOW TO USE THE MANTRAS

*E*ach mantra serves as a grounding point; a place to return to, to remind ourselves that our thoughts and emotions, colour all of our perceptions, including and especially those relating to wealth and abundance.

Each mantra has been written to remind you, and help you to remember your own inherent worthiness and value.

Each introduction aims to begin by meeting you where you are, in your current state of mind.

From there, the narrative serves to help you understand that a shift of perspective, no matter how tiny, is possible.

It takes you on a journey and guides you through the thought process to a different view, a different perspective, and ultimately a different you.

Use each of the introductions to help you understand, where you are, how you feel, and to help you understand and accept that the beliefs and experiences that have coloured your life have made you, all of who you are.

Read each introduction with an **open heart**, and an **open mind**.

Each one of these introductions has been written specifically in order to meet you, and your state of mind, exactly where you are.

Beginning with a typical thought, perception or belief and then moving on from there to an alternative, different perspective.

Each introduction gently guides you to a new awareness that there is a different, better way of looking at and dealing with the typical thoughts, ideas and beliefs that currently fill your mind and your being.

As you say each mantra for the first time, perhaps you might feel a little peculiar; a little strange as it gives voice to a new perspective of Truth.

These mantras may be far removed from the typical thoughts and beliefs that currently hold your attention, but reading, saying and repeating them will give you a new perspective in to what will be true, after all, remember…

We choose ALL of our own beliefs.

Persist.

Gradually as you repeat the mantra and feel more accustomed to it, feel wholly and completely devoted to the Truth that is verbalised within those little lines.

Feel the gratitude and appreciation of the Universe and all that surrounds you for the person that YOU are.

Throughout the week, every time you feel a thought that is 'less than', or find yourself on the verge of telling the version of a story that is focused on an unwanted or undesired story or experience, remind yourself of the mantra and repeat it; silently or verbally - whichever suits best, until you find yourself fully immersed in the emotions of your true **worth** and **value**

More than you know, greater than you can ever imagine.

A PERSONAL NOTE AND A GIFT

We have thoroughly enjoyed writing and creating this book for you, all the more so because it has been a very personal journey.

With each and every one of these mantras, we are sending out the very best of ourselves; our thoughts, hopes and wishes to you, embracing you as only the very best friends can, and wishing you a life filled with magic, joy and infinite abundance.

With love and joy,
Li-ling and Sam

To help you on your Year of Money and Abundance, we have created an accompanying workbook to help you get the most out of this book.

To download your free companion PDF workbook, please sign up at www.lilingooi.com/ayma

MANTRA 1

Money flows to me quickly, easily and abundantly; and I know that I am deserving and open to receiving it all.

MANTRA 1: INTRODUCTION

Money flows to me quickly, easily and abundantly; and I know that I am deserving and open to receiving it all.

With the mantra 'Money flows to me quickly, easily and abundantly; and I know that I am deserving and open to receiving it all' we focus on the abundance of money in and around the world.

As we contemplate the cyclic role that money plays in the world economy and our individual circumstances, we begin to understand that it flows as streams do, continuously and abundantly.

And slowly as we begin to accept and embrace the understanding that we are ultimately solely responsible for everything and anything that comes in to our experience and as such we are ready and deserving of all the abundance that comes our way.

As you say the first part of this mantra: money flows to me quickly, easily and abundantly – feel how this could be true. See the abundance of money and wealth in all its different forms filling your life, filling your wallets, filling your pockets, feel excited and happy in the knowing that wealth and abundance is continuously flowing to you.

As you sit and embrace this feeling of abundance that surrounds you, say the second part of the mantra: and I know that I am deserving and open to receiving it all.

As you say this, imagine the visual image of abundance however you imagine that to be whether a stream of gold light, or white light, a waterfall of wealth and money, surrounding and enveloping you. Feel its warmth and its blanket-like security surrounding you, protecting you and accept how deserving and worthy you are to receiving it all.

Money flows to me quickly, easily and abundantly; and I know that I am deserving and open to receiving it all.

MANTRA 2

I see opportunities everywhere and even though I may not be ready to embrace them yet; I know that this is just the beginning of an exciting, well-deserved journey to financial abundance.

MANTRA 2: INTRODUCTION

I see opportunities everywhere and even though I may not be ready to embrace them yet; I know that this is just the beginning of an exciting, well-deserved journey to financial abundance.

The mantra 'I see opportunities everywhere and even though I may not be ready to embrace them yet; I know that this is just the beginning for an exciting, well-deserved journey to financial abundance' helps us focus on the immense number of opportunities that continuously fill our existence and experience.

Each and every one of us has a numerous number of possible paths open at any one time, and in every moment of awareness, we are making choices and decisions, clothes to wear, food to eat, where to go, simple opportunities that we often take for granted.

As we focus on how these opportunities are completely open to us, we also begin to open ourselves to the greater larger opportunities - the life-changing ones.

Dreams of travelling round the world.
Dreams of running your own business
Dreams of working from home

As you repeat the mantra 'I see opportunities everywhere' - feel how exciting, fulfilling and easy it is to tune in to your dream or dreams, how opportunities are going to continuously come knocking for you.

Perhaps you may not be able to act on these yet, but take them as a sign that things are continuously working out in your favour.

As you visualise and emotionally tune in to the excitement and opportunities that abound, remind yourself how worthy and deserving you are of all that comes your way.

I see opportunities everywhere and even though I may not be ready to embrace them yet; I know that this is just the beginning of an exciting, well-deserved journey to financial abundance.

MANTRA 3

*I always have enough
money to do with all that I want and desire.*

MANTRA 3: INTRODUCTION

I always have enough money to do with all that I want and desire.

With this mantra, we begin to focus completely on the feelings and emotions of having enough. Having enough, not in the limiting sense, not in the sense of 'lowering expectations' or in the resigned feeling of letting things be...but in the feeling of excitement and knowing that somehow everything that you need, want or desire will be provided for - somehow.

We are all familiar with the experience of desiring something material. Greatly desiring; a beautiful piece of jewellery, a car, a gorgeous house...and then realising that it is out of reach because of its high cost and expense.

As you repeat the mantra, I always have enough money to do with all that I want and desire, feel the excitement of possibilities bubble up within, feel the expansion of opportunities open out in front of you, embrace the feeling of certainty that everything you want and desire is on its way to you.

Reach deep down for the feeling of contentment, of joy, for satisfaction, the feelings of gratitude and of appreciation and of knowing that the things you desire, are just around the corner.

I always have enough money to do with all that I want and desire.

MANTRA 4

Every little step that I take is helping me move closer towards achieving my goals.

MANTRA 4: INTRODUCTION

Every little step that I take is helping me move closer towards achieving my goals.

With the mantra 'Every little step that I take is helping me move closer towards achieving my goals' we consider the actions that we **believe** we need to take in order to achieve our goals and desires.

It is a very common for us all to assume that we are not doing enough or working hard enough to accomplish our heart's desire. We have come to define our achievements and accomplishments by the amount of work required – the number of hours, the number of effort-full days, the number of breaks and meals missed, the number of years spent plodding.

As you remember and repeat the mantra – 'every little step I take is helping me move closer towards achieving my goals', acknowledge that success and achievement takes more than just hard work. Beyond the actual working on your goal - every break, every cup of coffee, every moment of taking a breath, relaxing for a while, every acknowledgement of the great journey you've already travelled and progress already made, moves you closer to your goal.

As you make our way through this week, think about all the goals you would like to achieve and focus on the little steps. Remember to acknowledge and embrace each and every little action, no matter how insignificant it may seem; for

Every little step that I take is helping me move closer towards achieving my goals.

MANTRA 5

Every day that I live, I learn and gain more with each passing moment.

MANTRA 5: INTRODUCTION

Every day that I live, I learn and gain more with each passing moment.

The mantra 'Every day that I live, I learn and gain more with each passing moment' reminds us that we are never still in this journey through life.

It aims to help us focus on the present moment where we recognize the all amazing wonderful gifts that come our way with each passing moment, gifts that we rarely acknowledge and we hardly ever consider. Every single moment, offers us an opportunity to embrace a new experience, a new way of thinking, a new way of being.

As you travel through this week, when you find yourself pausing for a moment, acknowledge that you have progressed a little bit more – whether in experience, or in accomplishment, in the calm practice of mindfulness, and in every stage of life.

Find in yourself an appreciation for the journey you are making and embrace all that you experience. Remind yourself that every single experience serves to contribute to your greater being.

As you repeat the mantra this week, 'Every day that I live, I learn and gain more with each passing moment' acknowledge with gratitude and great appreciation all of the encounters and all of the engagements and experiences that your day brings.

Know and embrace that each moment, brings us to a new level of understanding, greater clarity and more wisdom.

Every day that I live, I learn and gain more with each passing moment.

MANTRA 6

I am contributing in valuable ways to everything and everyone around.

MANTRA 6: INTRODUCTION

I am contributing in valuable ways to everything and everyone around.

In the mantra 'I am contributing in valuable ways to everything and everyone around me' we focus on self-worth.

Often, we ourselves are prone to being the harshest judge of our own thoughts and actions where we unwittingly berate ourselves on a continuous basis with our self-talk and mentally criticize our physical appearance and our choices.

While we often think that any form of contribution requires a large action, a donation or a sacrifice in some way or another, we often overlook the most meaningful of contributions; a smile to a stranger who appears to be having a bad day, giving up a seat on the bus for someone in greater need, a penny (or maybe more) dropped in the hat of a homeless person and perhaps most valuable of all, a silent wish for the well-being and happiness of each and every person whose path you may cross.

As you repeat the mantra 'I am contributing in valuable ways to everything and everyone around me', recognise that you, play an enormous part in the lives of many others, your family, your colleagues, your company, your community, no matter how insignificant you think that role may be.

Your presence, your confidence, your quiet acknowledgement of all that is right around you contributes in ways far greater than you can imagine to all around you.

I am contributing in valuable ways to everything and everyone around me

MANTRA 7

I am deserving of all the wealth and prosperity that flows to me.

MANTRA 7: INTRODUCTION

I am deserving of all the wealth and prosperity that flows to me.

In the mantra 'I am deserving of all the wealth and prosperity that flows to me' we begin to acknowledge our self-worth in relation to wealth and prosperity.

Finding money on the pavement or a dollar note in a forgotten purse is often a source of great surprise and typically brings on a silent rendition of gratitude.

As a society we believe in the sanctity of hard work. We believe that rewards are distributed for efforts contributed. We have learned to trust that wealth and prosperity are simply a result of hard work – the harder the work the greater the rewards. While it may be that we do all need to contribute, to share our experiences, our skills, our gifts, we must also learn to embrace our very own, inherent self-worth.

As you repeat the mantra: 'I am deserving of all the wealth and prosperity that flows to me', feel deep down the well of appreciation that the entire Universe has for you, for your contributions, for your actions, and especially for your being.

The rewards, all in place for you, for your wealth and your prosperity, are on their way in more ways that you can imagine, simply because YOU are of the greatest value.

I am deserving of all the wealth and prosperity that flows to me.

MANTRA 8

Today, I know, that I am valuable and worthy of all the good that comes my way.

MANTRA 8: INTRODUCTION

Today, I know, that I am valuable and worthy of all the good that comes my way.

In the mantra 'Today, I know, that I am valuable and worthy of all the good that comes my way', we acknowledge with gratitude and appreciation all of the opportunities and experiences that happen throughout the day.

We often trudge through our days, every day, eyes closed in ignorance to the many positive experiences that actually cross our path. Caught up in our daily buzz and bustle, we have become oblivious to the small interactions that remind us of the worthiness of our lives – the knowing smile of a stranger, entertaining conversations with colleagues, the amazing progress of a child, the hug of a partner, the wet, sloppy kiss of a pet…

As you repeat the mantra 'Today, I know, that I am valuable and worthy of all the good that comes my way' acknowledge that your life is filled with wonderful and amazing experiences the gorgeous scent of a flower, the soothing warble of birdsong – our days are filled with an abundance of these small often seemingly insignificant joys.

Today, begin by acknowledging and embracing every single one of these, by reminding yourself that each and every one of these experiences are for you, and you alone and that you are treasured and adored, and most deserving of all of these wonderful gifts and more.

Today, I know, that I am valuable and worthy of all the good that comes my way.

MANTRA 9

Abundance abounds in everything that surrounds me, even financial wealth.

MANTRA 9: INTRODUCTION

Abundance abounds in everything that surrounds me, even financial wealth.

As we look around in our environments, we see that Abundance truly surrounds us in every way.

Nature naturally provides in abundance from the leaves on the trees to the vast landscapes, from the bountiful ocean life to the deep dense forests, in our cityscapes we are surrounded by feats of architecture and engineering, high rise buildings, vehicles of every shape, extensive connected roadways – in so many ways we are completely surrounded by various forms of abundance.

As you repeat the mantra 'Abundance abounds in everything that surrounds me, even financial wealth', embrace this abundance around you, revel in all of it and find yourself in awe and appreciation of it all.

Embrace this never-ending sense of out-pouring, of continual contribution from nature, from your surroundings, from the people around you. Feel how all of it consistently and continuously contributes to your well-being and greater wealth. Trust that you too, are entitled and deserving of every good thing that comes your way.

Abundance abounds in everything that surrounds me, even financial wealth.

MANTRA 10

I know and trust that Abundance will always flow my way.

MANTRA 10: INTRODUCTION

I know and trust that Abundance will always flow my way.

The mantra 'I know and trust that Abundance will always flow my way' talks to our faith in desiring and in allowing.

In so much of our daily lives, we focus on the things we lack, whether it is money, an object, an experience or other desires as yet unfulfilled. We tend to see and concentrate on the absence of our longings and forget that much of what we already have is a direct result of our abilities, accomplishments and allowing.

We, as adults, have generally forgotten what it is like to trust, to believe in the inherent goodness of all that surrounds us.

As you repeat the mantra 'I know and trust that Abundance will always flow my way', call upon that faithful knowing, the inherent emotional aspect of trust that all of us have, deep down. Tune in to that sense of releasing control, of letting go.

Revel in the wonderful abundance that already surrounds you and find, deep within, that remarkable sense of peace that comes with relinquishing control and embracing trust. Open up to receiving all the good that is ready to come to you.

I know and trust that Abundance will always flow my way.

MANTRA 11

The Universe always finds a way to give me all that I desire.

MANTRA 11: INTRODUCTION

The Universe always finds a way to give me all that I desire.

The mantra 'The Universe always finds a way to give me all that I desire' helps us embrace that part of us that is excited and accustomed to expecting and wanting more – more than our current situation offers.

When we find ourselves in that state of hoping or wishing for more, for better and for different things, very often a little voice creeps in and questions our worthiness and our deservability.

We begin to second-guess ourselves and often we relinquish desires because we deem ourselves unworthy of them.

As you repeat the mantra: 'The Universe always finds a way to give me all that I desire', feel yourself embrace the unknown, treat every desire – whether a physical object or a life experience – as if it were a walk through a forest, filled with surprises and unexpected gifts at every turn, the path may not always be smooth and sometimes, blind corners may seem scary, but ultimately the joy of the experience makes the destination all the more worthwhile.

Know with certainty that everything and everyone is collaborating to contribute to all that you wish.

The Universe always finds a way to give me all that I desire.

MANTRA 12

Money comes to me in more ways than I can imagine, I always trust and believe that it does.

MANTRA 12: INTRODUCTION

Money comes to me in more ways than I can imagine, I always trust and believe that it does.

The mantra 'Money comes to me in more ways than I can imagine, I always trust and believe that it does' speaks to our relationship with money – perceptions, thoughts and beliefs surrounding money.

All of us have fixed ideas about how and what money does and how it comes to us – typically we believe, through sacrifice and hard work. What we tend to overlook is that, a penny on the street or a winning lottery ticket, a free gift or a great experience, money and its value in all its various forms are available at all times in unlimited ways.

Our own limiting beliefs about the possibilities of how money can reach us, significantly limits our own opportunities for abundance.

As you repeat the mantra 'Money comes to me in more ways than I can imagine, I always trust and believe that it does' feel excited about the endless possibilities of finding money and great value throughout your day. Open up to all possibilities no matter how remote they may seem, a fleeting thought, a spark of a day dream, an inspiration to act, a calling to connect, so many possibilities abound.

Money comes to me in more ways than I can imagine, I always trust and believe that it does.

MANTRA 13

I have an unlimited tap on wealth and I am so happy, eager and excited to spend and share my good fortune with others.

MANTRA 13: INTRODUCTION

I have an unlimited tap on wealth and I am so happy, eager and excited to spend and share my good fortune with others.

The mantra 'I have an unlimited tap on wealth and I am so happy, eager and excited to spend and share my good fortune with others' emphasizes two separate aspects of our relationship with wealth; the first redefines our very own perception and perspective of wealth while the second taps into its influence on our behavior and desires as individuals and as members of a community.

It is a matter of fact that every one of us has unlimited potential, including the potential of wealth by being open to all options and embracing all possibilities, while the desire to extend a helping hand and to make a difference by contributing is innate in all of us.

As you say the first part of the mantra 'I have an unlimited tap on wealth', feel yourself open up to all possibilities, ready to embrace different opportunities, ready to revel in the shower of unlimited wealth and abundance. Feel the gurgling, bubbling well of excitement, deep within as you tune in to and embrace the limitless possibilities of wealth in your life.

As you repeat the second part of the mantra 'I am so happy, eager and excited to spend and share my good fortune with others' feel the joy, pleasure and satisfaction as you see yourself contributing in all the different ways that you can – a pleasing smile, a generous thought, a helping prayer, material contributions. Every little contribution is a contribution nonetheless.

I have an unlimited tap on wealth and I am so happy, eager and excited to spend and share my good fortune with others.

MANTRA 14

I live with great appreciation for all the opportunities and financial abundance that flow in to my life.

MANTRA 14: INTRODUCTION

I live with great appreciation for all the opportunities and financial abundance that flow in to my life.

The mantra 'I live with great appreciation for all the opportunities and financial abundance that flow in to my life' reminds us to focus on the good.

For most of our lives we pay attention to its challenges and difficulties. As a society, we are naturally more inclined to talk about 'what's going wrong' than to share the joys and successes within our own lives. In doing so, we tend to forget that within the myriad of experiences that make up our day, a great deal of it is filled with positive moments.

As you repeat the mantra this week, 'I live with great appreciation for all the opportunities and financial abundance that flow in to my life' focus first on all of the wonderful, amazing experiences that have already occurred in your life.

Fill up with and feel gratitude and appreciation for all the aspects of your life that are currently going well.

Then, focus on the amazing, never-ending possibilities that are constantly and continuously coming to you.

Stay open and excited about the opportunities that are just around the corner, new people, new experiences, new adventures.

I live with great appreciation for all the opportunities and financial abundance that flow in to my life.

MANTRA 15

I love knowing that the Universe has got my back, in everything that I desire and do.

MANTRA 15: INTRODUCTION

I love knowing that the Universe has got my back, in everything that I desire and do.

When we look back to when we were young as children, among the many memories of joy and fun, we also undoubtedly recall feeling secure, safe and being taken care of; we instinctively knew that someone was always looking out for us.

As we grew up, taking on more responsibilities, we began to learn that we needed to be responsible, independent and self-sufficient; we slowly but surely lost our ability to 'Trust'.

This week as you repeat the mantra 'I love knowing that the Universe has got my back, in everything that I desire and do', recall the feeling of joy and of being carefree, that you had as a child.

Remember what it was like to know with ease and confidence that things were being taken care of, that all you needed to be was exactly who you were.

This week, as far as you can, relinquish control and tune in to the Trust that is truly prevalent in many, many ways all around you.

I love knowing that the Universe has got my back, in everything that I desire and do.

MANTRA 16

The flow of Abundance and Wealth for me, is like a river flowing to the sea, unstoppable, undeniable and assured of its path and purpose.

MANTRA 16: INTRODUCTION

The flow of Abundance and Wealth for me, is like a river flowing to the sea, unstoppable, undeniable and assured of its path and purpose.

The mantra 'The flow of Abundance and Wealth for me, is like a river flowing to the sea, unstoppable, undeniable and assured of its path and purpose' helps to remind us to live in the flow.

The way our lives, and income are set up, that monthly paycheck, the bills, the fees, the expenses, it seems as if things come in limited blocks rather than the free-flowing, limitless stream that it could be; that it really is.

As our logical mind works towards the next paycheck, or the next appointment, we relinquish our ability to live in the state of 'flow'.

It takes conscious resolve to tune in to the state of mind that emphasizes the abundance that surrounds us and accept it as a part of our own journey.

As you say the mantra 'The flow of Abundance and Wealth for me, is like a river flowing to the sea, unstoppable, undeniable and assured of its path and purpose' tune in the flow of the water in a river. See in your mind's eye, the continuous, free flowing, unstoppable river of abundance and wealth.

Stay in that moment of flow and for as long as you can, and let the feeling of the continuity of abundance and wealth wash all over you.

The flow of Abundance and Wealth for me, is like a river flowing to the sea, unstoppable, undeniable and assured of its path and purpose.

MANTRA 17

Prosperity is my birthright. I am deserving of all the wealth, health and happiness that is to come my way.

MANTRA 17: INTRODUCTION

Prosperity is my birthright. I am deserving of all the wealth, health and happiness that is to come my way.

The mantra 'Prosperity is my birthright. I am deserving of all the wealth, health and happiness that is to come my way' speaks to our true natural state of being.

Little do we realize or recall that at the moment of birth, we are inherently surrounded by limitless potential and possibility; one in which prosperity is assured.

As we grow, in age and in experience, we begin to put in our own way a multitude of reasons that start us down the path of limitations. Questions such as 'who's feelings do I need to consider' and 'what I should be doing instead of…', the 'what if's' and 'why not's', our own silent self-talk is typical of the limitations that we place on our own path.

To begin moving away from this mindset, we have to recognise and then relinquish the fears, worries and limitations that we conjure up within ourselves. After that, we can begin to acknowledge and embrace our inherent worthiness.

As you repeat the mantra this week 'Prosperity is my birthright. I am deserving of all the wealth, health and happiness that is to come my way' recognise and remember that prosperity is yours to choose and to expect.

Tune in to your inherent worthiness and acknowledge, and accept that you too are deserving of every good thing that comes your way.

Wealth, health and happiness are not mere pipe dreams but are very real necessities in this life, necessities, that you more than deserve.

Sit for a moment as your repeat this mantra and let its words and truth wash over you.

Prosperity is my birthright. I am deserving of all the wealth, health and happiness that is to come my way.

MANTRA 18

Money comes to me in ways that are both expected and unexpected and I eagerly receive it.

MANTRA 18: INTRODUCTION

Money comes to me in ways that are both expected and unexpected and I eagerly receive it.

The mantra this week 'Money comes to me in ways that are both expected and unexpected and I eagerly receive it' speaks to our ability to accept and allow.

Through our logical mind we plan and we strategise, then we organise and we execute. We attempt to pre-empt and control every aspect of life in order to determine a desired outcome. We often leave as little room to the unknown as we can.

This is much the same of our attitude towards money. We watch our incomes, track our bills and expenditure, we do all that we can to maximise the former and minimise the latter. In all of this though, we leave little room for joyful surprises, for mysterious good fortunes and exciting finds.

As you repeat the mantra 'Money comes to me in ways that are both expected and unexpected and I eagerly receive it' think of the simple gorgeous flower in bloom, or the unexpected penny magically found by your feet; revel in the amazing dinner invitation from close friends and know our lives are filled with a host of unbelievable good fortune and exciting experiences and opportunities, simply be aware and open to them.

Open yourself to all possibilities and know that 'Money comes to me in ways that are both expected and unexpected and I eagerly receive it'.

MANTRA 19

Every single thing that I do is moving me closer to my goals.

MANTRA 19: INTRODUCTION

Every single thing that I do is moving me closer to my goals.

The mantra 'Every single thing that I do is moving me closer to my goals' aims to reconcile the different aspects of our lives that we compartmentalise into 'progress' and 'time-traps'.

Throughout our journey in life, we are typically aware that the things we do and the actions we take are either moving us towards or goals or keeping us away from it.

We like to believe that the more time we spend in front of our computer, or with our notebooks planning, detailing and optimising is vital for progress. In our action driven world, anything short of actual 'action' is a form of failure.

Sleeping, eating, down time, rest, tea and coffee breaks, each has been considered 'a waste of time'. It may be hard to believe that each one of these activities, no matter how seemingly pointless, actually moves us closer to our goals.

Consider the body builder who spends eight hours a day at the gym working out. Sleep, rest and good food are also essential components to his overall goal, without which his body would never have the time to recover from the stress it goes through and build the muscles it needs to.

As you repeat the mantra 'Every single thing that I do is moving me closer to my goals' acknowledge that every break, every moment's rest and unplanned diversion contributes in its own way to moving you closer to your goal.

Instead of the typical twinge of frustration or annoyance well, greet every seeming set back with a smile and a message of thanks in remembering that 'Every single thing that I do is moving me closer to my goals'.

MANTRA 20

I am worthy of all the best that life has to offer me.

MANTRA 20: INTRODUCTION

I am worthy of all the best that life has to offer me.

In the mantra 'I am worthy of all the best that life has to offer me' we focus on our self-worth and value and on the reckoning that throughout our lives, we embrace and accept the very best that comes our way.

Typically, in our life experiences, we find it difficult to acknowledge that we are deserving and worthwhile. Compliments are often hastily brushed aside and success modestly attributed to good luck.

We rarely, if ever, acknowledge that good things and experiences come our way because we deserve them. 'A fluke', we say, 'Aw, that was nothing'.

We attempt to play down any success or achievement, in part, because we mistakenly assume that we may help another feel better about their lack of triumph, but in reality, by doing so we merely beat down our own self-worth.

Beginning with this very moment, start to acknowledge that 'I am worthy of all the best that life has to offer me'. Understand that every beautiful, worthwhile experience is not simply chance, good luck or a fluke; it is a sign in every possible way that you are deserving of it.

Acknowledge and appreciate that 'I am worthy of all the best that life has to offer me' and life will always offer you its very best.

MANTRA 21

It is not the doing that counts, but the being... and Today I am being the best of me and I am open and ready to receive the best that the Universe can bring me.

MANTRA 21: INTRODUCTION

It is not the doing that counts, but the being... and Today I am being the best of me and I am open and ready to receive the best that the Universe can bring me.

The mantra 'It is not the doing that counts, but the being... and Today I am being the best of me and I am open and ready to receive the best that the Universe can bring me' focuses upon our very human obsession with doing.

Much of our lives are spent with the belief that we need to work, to do, to perform, to create and produce. And while it is not entirely untrue, we often forget that more than just doing we need also to learn to 'be'.

'Being' more than anything is a state of mind and to be the best of ourselves means opening up to our vulnerabilities, accepting and loving ourselves exactly as we are.

As you say the first part of the mantra 'It is not the doing that counts, but the being' begin letting go of the belief that results come only through action and gently feel yourself relinquish the need to do. Relax in to your own being.

'and Today I am being the best of me and I am open and ready to receive the best that the Universe can bring me' fill your heart with trust, appreciation and love for yourself and know that you are worthy of all the good things that come your way.

It is not the doing that counts, but the being… and Today I am being the best of me and I am open and ready to receive the best that the Universe can bring me.

MANTRA 22

As much as I can wish, desire and hope for, I know that I am worthy and deserving of receiving it all.

MANTRA 22: INTRODUCTION

As much as I can wish, desire and hope for, I know that I am worthy and deserving of receiving it all.

The mantra 'As much that I can wish, desire and hope for, I know that I am worthy and deserving of receiving it all' aims to reconcile our frequently felt guilt of wanting and desiring more.

From a young age we are taught that wanting more is a selfish desire. We are reminded that there are those less fortunate and that we should be content and grateful with all that we already have.

While it is always good to be grateful and appreciative of all you have achieved and where you are in life, it is never wrong to want or desire more and better for yourself.

As you repeat the mantra 'As much as I can wish, desire and hope for, I know that I am worthy and deserving of receiving it all' recognise that every thing you can imagine and wish for, you are deserving off.

Know that regardless of all that you already have, you are still entitled to more; greater dreams, more fun and bigger adventures.

Feel the avalanche of goodness and greatness, simply waiting to contribute to your every desire. Recognise that great worth within you and how much value you contribute simply by being you.

As much as I can wish, desire and hope for, I know that I am worthy and deserving of receiving it all.

MANTRA 23

Today, I am ready to receive all the blessings that the Universe can bestow upon me, knowing that I do not have to do or be anything other than the unique individual I already am.

MANTRA 23: INTRODUCTION

Today, I am ready to receive all the blessings that the Universe can bestow upon me, knowing that I do not have to do or be anything other than the unique individual I already am.

The mantra 'Today, I am ready to receive all the blessings that the Universe can bestow upon me, knowing that I do not have to do or be anything other than the unique individual I already am' speaks to the part of ourselves that challenges the belief that we are worthy, simply as we are.

All of us have a little voice within that attempts to convince us at every turn that there is always something more that we can do, a better way that we can be. It persuades us that good things happen only to deserving people; the people who have 'done the work', not us.

For some of us this voice is louder, while for others, through years of practice and training we have managed to soften or even neutralise it.

As you say the mantra 'Today, I am ready to receive all the blessings that the Universe can bestow upon me, knowing that I do not have to do or be anything other than the unique individual I already am' feel yourself relinquish the need and desire to judge yourself and your actions.

Wrap yourself up in a soothing blanket of 'enough' and embrace all the beautiful, wondrous moments expected and surprising that the Universe will bring to you today.

'Today, I am ready to receive all the blessings that the Universe can bestow upon me, knowing that I do not have to do or be anything other than the unique individual I already am'.

MANTRA 24

I love knowing and trusting that all good things are coming to me, in their own way, in their own time. All I have to do is prepare myself for receiving it all.

MANTRA 24: INTRODUCTION

I love knowing and trusting that all good things are coming to me, in their own way, in their own time. All I have to do is prepare myself for receiving it all.

One of the most difficult things to do in our journey through life is to relinquish control; to take a step back and acknowledge that sometimes letting go and trusting that things will work out is the best thing to do.

We are programmed to believe that things will happen only when we take action. And to add to that, we now live in a world, at a time where the hands of the ticking clock dictate almost all of the facets of our lives.

In much the same way, we have learnt to put our wants and desires on a stopwatch; defining when we need to have or do a certain thing; a deadline on achieving a certain goal.

As you say the mantra "I love knowing and trusting that all good things are coming to me, in their own way, in their own time. All I have to do is prepare myself for receiving it all" feel yourself relax and slowly relinquish control with every repetition.

In that space between your head and your heart, seek out the calm, gentle feeling of confident trust and embrace the beauty of each day as it unfolds moment by moment.

I love knowing and trusting that all good things are coming to me, in their own way, in their own time. All I have to do is prepare myself for receiving it all.

MANTRA 25

Everyone that surrounds me, tells a story of abundance, success, joy and happiness. I love being and knowing that I am a vital part of all those stories.

MANTRA 25: INTRODUCTION

Everyone that surrounds me, tells a story of abundance, success, joy and happiness. I love being and knowing that I am a vital part of all those stories.

The mantra 'Everyone that surrounds me, tells a story of abundance, success, joy and happiness. I love being and knowing that I am a vital part of all those stories' reminds us to look beyond the exterior surfaces of the people that we meet and encounter each day.

Being trained as we are to spot deficiencies and pick out faults, we miss the best and greatest things about each person we encounter. We easily miss the strong, stoic smile hidden underneath a coating of sarcasm. We callously overlook the determined strength required simply to get up each day.

We forget in our haste to rush through the day, all the people who have helped us through, from the lady at the supermarket checkout, to the college student barista.

As you repeat the mantra 'Everyone that surrounds me, tells a story of abundance, success, joy and happiness. I love being and knowing that I am a vital part of all those stories' remind yourself to look deep within each person you encounter and see the beauty of each one. Remember that all the best that you see is but a mere reflection of your own beauty within.

Go beyond the ragged exterior and look deep within; for within each one that you encounter, you will find a cavern of bounties, of jewels and riches, of kindness and of love.

Everyone that surrounds me, tells a story of abundance, success, joy and happiness. I love being and knowing that I am a vital part of all those stories.

MANTRA 26

No matter how much I falter, or how much I question the logic or sanity of giving up and trusting in the Universe, it always manages to find a way to show me that All is Well.

MANTRA 26: INTRODUCTION

No matter how much I falter, or how much I question the logic or sanity of giving up and trusting in the Universe, it always manages to find a way to show me that All is Well.

In the times when we are at our lowest, when it feels that all hope is lost and there is nothing left, it is only then that we are compelled to 'give up', to surrender and when we do, things often turn around quickly. More quickly that we can explain with our logic or reason.

As you say the mantra, 'No matter how much I falter, or how much I question the logic or sanity of giving up and trusting in the Universe, it always manages to find a way to show me that All is Well' feel the lightness grow within as you readily relinquish control, concern and worry.

Remind yourself of all the wonderful, amazing, small perhaps even insignificant, moments that consistently interject in to your day.

Notice every little thing that goes right and accept them as markers of an even greater goodness at play.

And remember, 'No matter how much I falter, or how much I question the logic or sanity of giving up and trusting in the Universe, it always manages to find a way to show me that All is Well'.

MANTRA 27

I live a life of infinite abundance because I am ready, willing and deserving of all that I desire.

MANTRA 27: INTRODUCTION

I live a life of infinite abundance because I am ready, willing and deserving of all that I desire.

The mantra 'I live a life of infinite abundance because I am ready, willing and deserving of all that I desire' helps us to look beyond the limitations that we place upon ourselves.

When we are ready to live in the space of acknowledging abundance, we begin to observe and notice that we are truly surrounded by abundance in a multitude of forms – the leaves on the trees, the vast open green, the limitless never-ending skies. From here we can begin to transfer and translate the perspective of abundance in to our own lives.

As you repeat the mantra 'I live a life of infinite abundance because I am ready, willing and deserving of all that I desire' acknowledge that abundance is already a part of your life, that there is infinite wealth and prosperity all ready for you.

The feeling of abundance comes to you as emotions of limitless joy, of acknowledging that you already live a sacred, fulfilled life.

Feel yourself secure in the knowing that you deserve every bit of goodness that comes your way and that more is around the corner.

I live a life of infinite abundance because I am ready, willing and deserving of all that I desire.

MANTRA 28

I love knowing that all the good things that I desire are coming my way.

MANTRA 28: INTRODUCTION

I love knowing that all the good things that I desire are coming my way.

The mantra 'I love knowing that all the good things that I desire are coming my way' aims to help us embrace a notion of certainty and confidence, of worthiness and value.

While we often claim 'I know', 'I know'; I know that good things are simply around the corner, I know that I deserve all the good that comes to us.

Most of the time, we are paying empty lip service with words that we hope will mask our own insecurity and self-doubt, usually, in an attempt to convince ourselves of its truth.

No more.

As you say the mantra, 'I love knowing that all the good things that I desire are coming my way' reach deep. Reach deep to the core of your being and remember the feeling of knowing and of trusting.

Remember learning to walk, knowing, knowing that with every step and every falter, it was all part of achieving a steady gait.

Recognise the deep belly confidence, the assured poise, the upright, shoulders back and head held high walk of knowing.

Knowing that you deserve all the very best, knowing that things are always working out, knowing that with every breath and every step forward all the best is on its way.

I love knowing that all the good things that I desire are coming my way.

MANTRA 29

With each day, in every little way, I am living my life in full appreciation of the abundance that surrounds me.

MANTRA 29: INTRODUCTION

With each day, in every little way, I am living my life in full appreciation of the abundance that surrounds me.

'With each day, in every little way, I am living my life in full appreciation of the abundance that surrounds me'.

From the moment we open our eyes in the morning to the time our head hits the pillow in sleep, we are focused on the happenings of our own corner of the world and beyond, we are conscious of our actions and inactions and often the day passes by in something of a blur as we almost robotically manoeuvre through it.

When we begin to awaken to the beauty and abundance that surrounds us in all its forms, we realise that there is much more to be found.

As you say the mantra 'With each day, in every little way, I am living my life in full appreciation of the abundance that surrounds me' acknowledge that there is abundance in your life that you have often missed.

Take note of things as simple as the stationery on your desk or the vast fields of grass on the ground, the multitude of cars in the street or flowers in the park and notice, notice that abundance abounds in more ways than we realise.

With every observation, acknowledge the presence of abundance, acknowledge with thanks the beauty and casual over-flowing in nature that reminds us that abundance surrounds and abounds all around, to you and for you.

With each day, in every little way, I am living my life in full appreciation of the abundance that surrounds me.

MANTRA 30

Wealth and abundance is my birthright and I love knowing that it is all working out exactly as it should.

MANTRA 30: INTRODUCTION

Wealth and abundance is my birthright and I love knowing that it is all working out exactly as it should.

The mantra 'Wealth and abundance is my birthright and I love knowing that it is all working out exactly as it should' reminds us that no matter what the circumstances of our birth or of our current situation the potential for wealth, for abundance, for all that we desire and deserve is here, right here in every moment that we acknowledge.

Often we look around us and we see through our slanted, selective lenses of limits, all that we do not yet have, and have not yet achieved; we are unwilling to easily acknowledge that where we currently stand is but a stepping-stone along the journey.

Surrounded by where we are and what we have, we are inclined to stop and take score often counting up, all that we do not yet have.

As you repeat the mantra, 'Wealth and abundance is my birthright and I love knowing that it is all working out exactly as it should' feel the out-pouring of abundance and of wealth in everything that surrounds you, for you and to you.

Feel and acknowledge with even greater appreciation that you are meant to be exactly where you are at this moment, and while things are moving in ways that you cannot see or begin to understand, they are always working out for you.

Wealth and abundance is my birthright and I love knowing that it is all working out exactly as it should.

MANTRA 31

I know that I am worthy of every thing that I desire and I know that things are always working out for me.

MANTRA 31: INTRODUCTION

I know that I am worthy of every thing that I desire and I know that things are always working out for me.

Often, when it takes a while for the things we want to come in to our experience, when it takes a little longer than expected to succeed, we naturally start to question our worthiness and begin to doubt our own desires.

In the end we relinquish the thought of ever wanting much less owning it. Giving up on desires and dreams are common as we talk ourselves in to believing 'Oh the timing wasn't right' or 'It just wasn't for me'.

As you say the mantra, 'I know that I am worthy of every thing that I desire and I know that things are always working out for me' acknowledge that even though it may take a while for the things you want to come to you, your desire for it is rooted in the vast depths of your worth and value.

You are able to want and to desire so much because it merely scratches the surface of all that you are worthy of. No desire is too much or too great for you because in each and every respect you are worthy and deserving of it all.

And through each step along the way, every thought, action and belief is rooted in the knowing that things are always going the right way.

I know that I am worthy of every thing that I desire and I know that things are always working out for me.

MANTRA 32

Financial abundance is simply a step in the right direction, a focus on the right thought, a smile to all that surrounds me.

MANTRA 32: INTRODUCTION

Financial abundance is simply a step in the right direction, a focus on the right thought, a smile to all that surrounds me.

The mantra 'Financial abundance is simply a step in the right direction, a focus on the right thought, a smile to all that surrounds me' aims to widen the scope of our perception and perspectives of financial abundance.

Even though, we have all heard stories of chance meetings, of accidents that lead to amazing collaboration and cooperation, it is difficult to imagine ourselves in those situations or circumstances.

All of us have convinced ourselves that financial abundance comes from hard work, and focusing on what we can do and all that we have to do.

And yet, when we leave room in our lives for surprise, for beauty, for fun and for joy, we begin to realise that it takes more than just hard work to move us along our journey.

As you say the mantra 'Financial abundance is simply a step in the right direction, a focus on the right thought, a smile to all that surrounds me' acknowledge that while work contributes in every way to greater financial wealth, it inevitably helps to be on the right path, moving in the right direction.

Feel how your every action, thought and emotion continuously contributes to your own financial abundance and with a simple smile, the thoroughness of appreciation in and for all things adds tremendously to the beauty of your journey.

Financial abundance is simply a step in the right direction, a focus on the right thought, a smile to all that surround me.

MANTRA 33

With each little thought, focus and choice, the Universe continues to show me how worthy I am.

MANTRA 33: INTRODUCTION

With each little thought, focus and choice, the Universe continues to show me how worthy I am.

The mantra 'With each little thought, focus and choice, the Universe continues to show me how worthy I am' helps us remember that it is not always in the large actions and visions that we see and feel a sense of our place in this world.

Each of us finds ourselves in a place in the world and a lot of the time, it is not how we imagine or even wish it to be. Yet as we embrace the beauty of all that lies around us, the warm, comfortable, familiar rooms of home, the joyful, rapturous song of a bird and in the wonder that we choose to focus on, we are reminded that beauty, joy and love surrounds us.

As you say the mantra, 'With each little thought, focus and choice, the Universe continues to show me how worthy I am', remember that every thought, action, and emotion is a choice.

Remind yourself that no matter what the circumstances, you can choose how you respond and in doing so, at every moment, choose to focus on all that pleases you. As you continue to do so, more and more will present itself for your appreciative awe.

With each little thought, focus and choice, the Universe continues to show me how worthy I am.

MANTRA 34

I know and trust that abundance is an undeniable part of my life and I am deserving of all the good things that comes with it.

MANTRA 34: INTRODUCTION

I know and trust that abundance is an undeniable part of my life and I am deserving of all the good things that comes with it.

It is so easy to believe, as we stand ourselves in comparison to our fellowman that they have done better, achieved more and live better lives. We convince ourselves of our lack on both physical and emotional terms, and yet, when we are able to stop for a moment to reflect on our own paths and journeys, we come to the realization that we too have been blessed.

The mantra 'I know and trust that abundance is an undeniable part of my life and I am deserving of all the good things that comes with it' focuses on helping us remember that we are surrounded by abundance in all forms.

It is undeniable in nature and in the world that we have built – from endless blue skies, vast seas of green fields, flowers in all shapes and forms to towering sky scrappers and never-ending road and train systems.

As you repeat the mantra 'I know and trust that abundance is an undeniable part of my life and I am deserving of all the good things that comes with it' feel yourself opening up to the already present abundance and endless opportunities present and continuously coming in to your life.

Recognise the joy and ease that comes with trusting that more is always on its way to you.

I know and trust that abundance is an undeniable part of my life and I am deserving of all the good things that comes with it.

MANTRA 35

Money is an amazing, never ending resource that continuously flows to me with ease and joy.

MANTRA 35: INTRODUCTION

Money is an amazing, never ending resource that continuously flows to me with ease and joy.

The mantra 'Money is an amazing, never ending resource that continuously flows to me with ease and joy' helps to find a new perspective on money.

Among one the greatest universal desires is to have enough money to live a life that is free and easy, yet on most accounts, we deem money to be difficult and often even evil. We believe that money is the cause of debt and greed, the root of wars and discord.

Yet the fact is, money on its own is completely innocuous. Money simply takes its power from our assigning to it, what we believe of its worth.

As you say the mantra 'Money is an amazing, never ending resource that continuously flows to me with ease and joy' recognise that money is a tool, a resource that works to make our lives convenient and easy.

Feel the freedom that money offers in its ability as a transcriber of goods and services. Notice the essence of flow in relation to money and recognise its ability to always work exactly as you require it to.

Money is an amazing, never ending resource that continuously flows to me with ease and joy.

MANTRA 36

I love knowing that I am always exactly in the right place at precisely the right time and that everything is always working out for me.

MANTRA 36: INTRODUCTION

I love knowing that I am always exactly in the right place at precisely the right time and that everything is always working out for me.

Our lives are littered with moments in which we wish that something was different, or that things would change. While not quite as strong as regret, we may often find ourselves in that space of wishing we had done something different or reacted differently.

It is but a small step to learning to accept that all that comes to pass is part and parcel of the journey; to bless each reaction and encounter as an experience that adds vibrance and colour to your life.

As you say the mantra 'I love knowing that I am always exactly in the right place at precisely the right time and that everything is always working out for me', close your eyes and feel peace settle in, and around you.

Embrace yourself and your journey, for everyone's is special and unique.

Feel the confidence build within as you tap in to the certainty that everything always works out, regardless of what others may say or think. The path is yours alone to walk, and with every step, doing well and feeling good are choices for you to make.

'I love knowing that I am always exactly in the right place at precisely the right time and that everything is always working out for me'.

MANTRA 37

I enjoy living life with ease and grace knowing that all that I desire is just around the corner.

MANTRA 37: INTRODUCTION

I enjoy living life with ease and grace knowing that all that I desire is just around the corner.

The mantra 'I enjoy living life with ease and grace knowing that all that I desire is just around the corner' focuses on how we can embrace expectation.

There is often a tinge of frustration that surrounds desire; impatience hot on the trails of what we want and what we feel we deserve. In every moment of rejecting, that where we are is part of the journey, we begin to feel the wells of discontent and dissatisfaction over-flow.

As you say the mantra 'I enjoy living life with ease and grace knowing that all that I desire is just around the corner' acknowledge that where you are is in perfect harmony with the entire orchestra of your creation.

Relax in to the knowing that no matter where you are in relation to where you want to be, at this present moment in time, life is good.

Embrace the gift of appreciation that together with the wonder of expectation provides a never-ending opportunity for wonderful adventures, beautiful journeys and magnificent accomplishments.

'I enjoy living life with ease and grace knowing that all that I desire is just around the corner.

MANTRA 38

I celebrate the success of each and every person because in their success I see the reflection and the becoming of all that I desire.

MANTRA 38: INTRODUCTION

I celebrate the success of each and every person because in their success I see the reflection and the becoming of all that I desire.

In our very human nature, even from a young age, we learn to see someone else's success as somehow limiting to our own. We find ourselves secretly wishing 'That should have been me'.

Yet unbeknown to us, this mindset and its related emotions, chip away at our ability to feel generous, to be magnanimous and at our ability to see the best in others and in ourselves.

As you say the mantra 'I celebrate the success of each and every person because in their success I see the reflection and the becoming of all that I desire' acknowledge that success is a vast well of opportunity that refills itself at every turn.

Revel in the success of another, just as you would if they were your own.

Feel the joy and happiness of achievement, on behalf of someone else.

Remember another's achievements does not diminish your own

abilities and capabilities, and to recognise that another's accomplishments simply provide a stepping-stone to greater triumphs of your own.

I celebrate the success of each and every person because in their success I see the reflection and the becoming of all that I desire.

MANTRA 39

I am so happy and excited to be able to live my life to the full fruition of all possibilities.

MANTRA 39: INTRODUCTION

I am so happy and excited to be able to live my life to the full fruition of all possibilities.

The mantra 'I am so happy and excited to be able to live my life to the full fruition of all possibilities' helps us embrace options, potentials and promises with joyous expectation.

Learning to stay in that state of joy and bliss regardless of where we currently stand is in part, a lesson in facing forward. To be able to look beyond our immediate environment and to acknowledge that no matter where we are right now, things are constantly changing and possibilities are always on their way.

Being able to embrace the exhilaration of the journey, and ride the excitement of all that is ahead offers us but a glimpse of the many wonders to come.

As you say the mantra 'I am so happy and excited to be able to live my life to the full fruition of all possibilities' feel the joyous fervor deep within the belly of your being.

Notice the gurgling, feverish excitement that accompanies expectation on the brink of becoming.

Embrace the lightness in your heart and spring in each step as you skip your way towards all that you desire, knowing deep within that it all begins with this tangible, perceptible emotion of happiness.

'I am so happy and excited to be able to live my life to the full fruition of all possibilities'

MANTRA 40

I embrace all the experiences that come my way and I know that each and every one contributes to the greater whole of me.

MANTRA 40: INTRODUCTION

I embrace all the experiences that come my way and I know that each and every one contributes to the greater whole of me.

As we move through our days taking stock and taking score of the good and the bad, we judge how each has colored us. We define the good as pleasurable, as that makes us happy while we lump the general displeasure, discontent and unhappiness in an unwanted pile, believing that we would have been far better off without those.

Little do we realize nor can we easily bring ourselves to admit, that each bitter pill that we are made to swallow, brings with it a multitude of greatness and goodness.

For each in its own way, helps us to acknowledge, to recognise and to allow, the vastness of our experience and all of the beauty that colours our lives.

As you say the mantra 'I embrace all the experiences that come my way and I know that each and every one contributes to the greater whole of me' take pleasure in knowing that all you have experienced is part and parcel of the beautiful, amazing person that you already are. Feel the pleasure and the contentment of embracing yourself exactly as you already are, knowing that with each passing moment and each coming experience you simply become more of who you were meant to be.

I embrace all the experiences that come my way and I know that each and every one contributes to the greater whole of me.

MANTRA 41

I am valuable in far more ways than I can imagine and the Universe is constantly finding ways to show me how much I am treasured.

MANTRA 41: INTRODUCTION

I am valuable in far more ways than I can imagine and the Universe is constantly finding ways to show me how much I am treasured.

The mantra 'I am valuable in far more ways than I can imagine and the Universe is constantly finding ways to show me how much I am treasured' helps us to recognise the value in all that we are and shows us how to embrace each experience as a gift specifically and only for us.

In each moment that we delight in the rapturous song of a bird, or feel our heart soar at the rising of the sun over a horizon of vast blue ocean; when we close our eyes and breathe in the wondrous perfume of a flower, or find ourselves floating on a cloud of beautiful music; in every one of these moments in which we attribute great appreciation for our world and all that surrounds us, we remember that each is a gift.

A gift to us, a gift for us; a gift that says 'You are so loved; and thank you. Thank you for being the perfect person that you already are'

As you say that mantra 'I am valuable in far more ways than I can imagine and the Universe is constantly finding ways to show me how much I am treasured' recognise that each day is filled with beauty, with song, with kindness and with pleasure.

Remind yourself that every little joy that lifts your heart is but a small reminder of the great treasure that you truly are.

I am valuable in far more ways than I can imagine and the Universe is constantly finding ways to show me how much I am treasured.

MANTRA 42

Wealth, health and happiness are my birthright and I feel an unparalleled joy and gratitude for each passing moment as it moves me closer to my dreams and desires.

MANTRA 42: INTRODUCTION

Wealth, health and happiness are my birthright and I feel an unparalleled joy and gratitude for each passing moment as it moves me closer to my dreams and desires.

The mantra 'Wealth, health and happiness are my birthright and I feel an unparalleled joy and gratitude for each passing moment as it moves me closer to my dreams and desires' reminds us that in our ability to hold happiness and appreciation in our hearts we bring ourselves closer to the gifts that each and every one of us are already born with.

Regardless of the circumstances of our background or of the details of our journey so far, each and every one of us is deserving of all of the desires we can dream of. In a multitude of ways, we hold ourselves apart from what we want simply by believing that we are not worthy or that we do not truly deserve what we want or it would have already become.

As you say the first part of the mantra 'Wealth, health and happiness are my birthright...' tune in to the deep-seated knowing in the truth, that wealth, health and happiness is your birthright and is yours for you always.

And as you say the second part 'and I feel an unparalleled joy and gratitude for each passing moment as it moves me closer to my dreams and desires' feel the welling up and the over-flowing sensation of gratitude and of appreciation for this beautiful, wondrous life that you already live. Know with certainty that each moment you spend in joyous jubilation lightens and clears the path, taking you to where you want to be.

Wealth, health and happiness are my birthright and I feel an unparalleled joy and gratitude for each passing moment as it moves me closer to my dreams and desires.

MANTRA 43

My heart is filled with love and appreciation and it reflects in my outer world.

MANTRA 43: INTRODUCTION

My heart is filled with love and appreciation and it reflects in my outer world.

The mantra 'My heart is filled with love and appreciation and it reflects in my outer world' reminds us that all things begin from within.

So much of our time is spent trying to control, trying to change our external world, from material wants and desires, to changes in physical location, all of us can think of things we want to change.

Yet, while we readily and intellectually acknowledge that whatever change we wish begins first with our internal processes, we rarely pause with sufficient time and purpose to put it in to practice.

As you repeat the mantra 'My heart is filled with love and appreciation and it reflects in my outer world' feel the words slowly descend from your head, in to your heart. Notice the calm that envelopes you as you begin to acknowledge that love and appreciation are both an integral part of your being.

Open yourself up to the beauty and magnificence of all that

already surrounds you; from the vast blue sky, to the wondrous vehicles that you travel in, from the simple, humble slice of toast to the beautiful, awe-inspiring landscapes that surround this world.

My heart is filled with love and appreciation and it reflects in my outer world.

MANTRA 44

All day every day, I embrace the thoughts, words and actions that fill me with the belief and the knowing that all good things are coming my way.

MANTRA 44: INTRODUCTION

All day every day, I embrace the thoughts, words and actions that fill me with the belief and the knowing that all good things are coming my way.

In every passing moment, we each have the ability, and the power, to choose the thoughts that make up our decisions, ideas, beliefs and emotions.

Often however, it feels as if we are simply the passive recipients of each thought, in which we have little control over how or when it 'comes' to us, but only that we have to respond to each one.

The mantra 'All day every day, I embrace the thoughts, words and actions that fill me with the belief and the knowing that all good things are coming my way' reminds us that in every moment, at every point, we have the capability to decide, to filter and to choose; to select and accept thoughts and responses that help us embrace the best of ourselves.

As you say the mantra 'All day every day, I embrace the thoughts, words and actions that fill me with the belief and the knowing that all good things are coming my way' acknowledge that you have the power over the thoughts that come to you.

Recognise that at every moment in time, with every thought that you think, you are prepared and ready to focus on the positive and on every little humble good that crosses the threshold in to your experience.

Feel the eagerness that drives you as you begin to count and acknowledge all of the beautiful, wonderful experiences that make up your day. Know that with every recognition of appreciation, that more is on its way.

All day every day, I embrace the thoughts, words and actions that fill me with the belief and the knowing that all good things are coming my way.

MANTRA 45

So much, so often, so valuable, so grateful, very much appreciated - these are the words that describe my feelings all day, every day.

MANTRA 45: INTRODUCTION

So much, so often, so valuable, so grateful, very much appreciated - these are the words that describe my feelings all day, every day.

The mantra 'So much, so often, so valuable, so grateful, very much appreciated - these are the words that describe my feelings all day, every day' helps us to recognise that in every moment of our daily lives we have much to be grateful and thankful for.

It is rare that we are fully cognizant or aware of the abundance, gifts and special privileges that make up our experience of life and of living. Our internal thermostat of emotions is so often routinely pointed to an acknowledgement of lack, focused squarely on desires that have not yet become evident.

As you say the mantra 'So much, so often, so valuable, so grateful, very much appreciated - these are the words that describe my feelings all day, every day' feel the out-pouring and over-flowing of all that is good in your life right now. Acknowledge that while, it may still be a little way to your ideal situation, there is much and more that is valuable right now than there was before.

Breathe in with ease and with certainty that so much, so often, so valuable is the perfect description of your journey as you stand with 'so grateful and very much appreciated' here and look forward in to the future.

So much, so often, so valuable, so grateful, very much appreciated - these are the words that describe my feelings all day, every day.

MANTRA 46

I love knowing that I am in charge of all that I can be and that the Universe is both the beacon that lights my way and the wind that carries me forward.

MANTRA 46: INTRODUCTION

I love knowing that I am in charge of all that I can be and that the Universe is both the beacon that lights my way and the wind that carries me forward.

The mantra 'I love knowing that I am in charge of all that I can be and that the Universe is both the beacon that lights my way and the wind that carries me forward', reminds us to tune in to the feeling of confidence and certainty that we are on the right path at every moment in time.

The game of second-guessing, of doubt and hesitation is one that is ever present in our every day lives. Somehow over the course of our life's journey, we have all, embedded messages and beliefs that teach us, not to trust our own sense and intuition, but to look for external approval and consent. We have been made to believe that in doing so, we inherently become a better member of society.

And yet at the same time, we recognise that in giving away our ability to decide what is good for us, rarely, feels correct. Living someone else's life, playing by someone else's rules, believing in someone else's dream; at best, makes us a reflection of their triumphs, at worse, forsakes completely, who we really are.

As you say the mantra 'I love knowing that I am in charge of all that I can be and that the Universe is both the beacon that lights my way and the wind that carries me forward' feel the confidence arise within you in the knowing, that you are a unique, special, amazing and beautiful person.

Sense the overwhelming approval of all at surrounds you, and at the acknowledgement given, to knowing, that you, and only you are capable and powerful enough to make decisions for you. Greet with magnanimous joy the realization that you are guided and supported every step of your path.

I love knowing that I am in charge of all that I can be and that the Universe is both the beacon that lights my way and the wind that carries me forward.

MANTRA 47

Financial abundance is a state of mind that tells me I am valuable and worthy of all that comes my way.

MANTRA 47: INTRODUCTION

Financial abundance is a state of mind that tells me I am valuable and worthy of all that comes my way.

The mantra 'Financial abundance is a state of mind that tells me I am valuable and worthy of all that comes my way' seeks to embed within us the understanding that financial abundance is less of a physical condition and more of a mindset.

The first step in any acknowledgement of wealth is the confidence and assurance that we are deserving of every bit of it; regardless of whether wealth is a result of back-breaking hard work, or a consequence of luck and providence; accepting that it is of value to us and for us, simply because we are worthy of accepting and receiving it.

In our learned perspectives of self-worth, many of the lessons have chipped away at our self-esteem, often revealing a vulnerable core that makes us question why we would be deserving at all.

As you say the mantra 'Financial abundance is a state of mind that tells me I am valuable and worthy of all that comes my way' accept that you are valuable and worthy simply as you are. Remember, no matter how small a piece of the jigsaw may be, any missing piece ruins the whole picture.

Take a deep breath and pause for a moment, to embrace the new understanding that every thing and every experience that crosses your path today, does so, not by simple fluke or chance, but because you are deserving of it; the smile from a stranger, the warm frothy coffee, hand-made by the barista, your favorite scarf or shirt, the music playing...

Recognise that every little experience of pleasure, joy and wonder, tells a story of greater good coming your way.

Financial abundance is a state of mind that tells me I am valuable and worthy of all that comes my way.

MANTRA 48

I know that I am deserving and worthy of everything I desire.

MANTRA 48: INTRODUCTION

I know that I am deserving and worthy of everything I desire.

In the fraction of time that it takes to second guess ourselves, we would have, in one fell swoop, decided that 'there are others more deserving', that 'our wants and longings are mere daydreams' and that 'we are fooling ourselves'.

The confidence and certainty it takes to 'know' is molded by a strong determination to embrace everything about ourselves – from our faults and our limits, to our best and brightest traits.

In order to embrace our desires and to not think ourselves greedy or undeserving, we also need to realize and accept that everyone is on their own path, and that no matter what attempts we may make to smooth the way for someone else, ultimately our only control is upon the destination of our choice.

As you say the mantra 'I know that I am deserving and worthy of everything I desire' tune in to the intellectual experience of knowing with certainty and the feeling of trust in yourself that comes from confidence in your thoughts, your decisions and your emotions.

Feel the deep-seated sense of peace that all is well and that in each moment of your reckoning, you are already deserving and worthy of all that already surrounds you and all that is coming your way.

I know that I am deserving and worthy of everything I desire.

MANTRA 49

I love knowing that deep within my heart, I have a never-ending trail of appreciation for everything that I experience, see and feel; and I know that good things will continue to unfold for me.

MANTRA 49: INTRODUCTION

I love knowing that deep within my heart, I have a never-ending trail of appreciation for everything that I experience, see and feel; and I know that good things will continue to unfold for me.

The mantra 'I love knowing that deep within my heart, I have a never-ending trail of appreciation for everything that I experience, see and feel and I know that good things will continue to unfold for me' helps us understand that there is an infinite link between the good that we are able to appreciate from the core of our being and that which is seen in the world around us.

No matter how harshly our times may have been on occasion; no matter how difficult it may be to reconcile experiences in our head to those that we know that we should focus on; when we tune in to the greater sense of who we are, when we are able to acknowledge, that beyond the surface of our physicality there is a deeper link that connects us to all things and all people; we uncover our innate sense of love and appreciation.

As you say the mantra 'I love knowing that deep within my heart, I have a never-ending trail of appreciation for everything that I experience, see and feel; and I know that good things will continue to unfold for me', reach deep in to the stillness within and find yourself basking in the out-pouring of kindness, contentment and appreciation for all that you are.

Feel the sense of ease and of serenity as you look around and remember, with joy in your heart and appreciation all around that there is nothing and no one as worthy as you.

I love knowing that deep within my heart, I have a never-ending trail of appreciation for everything that I experience, see and feel; and I know that good things will continue to unfold for me.

MANTRA 50

So many special moments, so many amazing experiences, so much abundance, all just for me.

MANTRA 50: INTRODUCTION

So many special moments, so many amazing experiences, so much abundance, all just for me.

The mantra 'So many special moments, so many amazing experiences, so much abundance, all for me' helps us remember and focus on the wonderful, remarkable encounters of every day living.

Each day of our lives is filled with a multitude of beautiful happenings, many of which we are rarely aware of, nor concerned or bothered with. From the simple, constant and consistent beating of our own heart, to the sound of rustling leaves on the tree, from the busy vibe in the bustle of a city street to the quiet, peaceful wonder of the setting sun; all day, every day is packed with numerous unique experiences.

Many of which, we overlook in our haste to focus on the things which are of 'greater importance', results of the workday, traffic on the road, outcomes of assessments, sales figures, final takes. As we take stock, and measure with our logical mind, we miss the inherent beauty and joy in the little things of everyday

As you say the mantra, 'So many special moments, so many amazing experiences, so much abundance, all for me' take a deep breath; and as you exhale feel the calm wash over you.

For a quiet moment, tune in to the part of you that remembers the joyous amazement in recognizing the wonder that surrounds you. Revel in the abundance that fills our world and acknowledge that all of it is for you, to you and is you.

So many special moments, so many amazing experiences, so much abundance, all for me

MANTRA 51

The one thing that is truly guaranteed in this amazing life of mine, is how worthy I am, of every good thing that comes my way.

MANTRA 51: INTRODUCTION

The one thing that is truly guaranteed in this amazing life of mine, is how worthy I am, of every good thing that comes my way.

The mantra 'The one thing that is truly guaranteed in this amazing life of mine, is how worthy I am, of every good thing that comes my way' encourages us to recognise and acknowledge that no matter where we have come from and no matter where we are going, it falls squarely on us, ourselves, to remember that ours is a worthy, wondrous life.

When something good, expected or unexpected occurs in our lives, often we respond in surprise, perhaps even relief. Rarely do we accept that we are deserving of it, or that it was not simply chance or luck but a predestined path of embracing our ever-growing sense of self-worth. Simply attributing good fortune, to luck and fate downplays the psychology of self-esteem and self-value.

As we, out of habit, represent the positive in our lives in terms of favors, presented by a power outside of ourselves (good luck), we begin to deny the perspective of our own value, of our own merits and of our own deserving.

As you say the mantra 'The one thing that is truly guaranteed in this amazing life of mine, is how worthy I am, of every good thing that comes my way' acknowledge that each victory and each triumph, no matter how small, as a sign and a symbol that you are deserving of all this and more, as you embrace every experience that crosses your path.

Feel how truly amazing it is to live in times of freedom of choice, of power of thought and progress, and of limitless opportunities. Love every small joy, embrace every little delight, and bask in the bliss of every day as it unfolds.

The one thing that is truly guaranteed in this amazing life of mine, is how worthy I am, of every good thing that comes my way.

MANTRA 52

It is so amazing to feel the flow of desire and abundance fill every pore of my being.

MANTRA 52: INTRODUCTION

It is so amazing to feel the flow of desire and abundance fill every pore of my being.

Through our experiences of life, it has become natural to fight against desires. In part because we have been taught that to desire and to want more is a selfish notion, but also because in the process of living, we learn to believe that if we want something too much, it becomes even more unlikely that we will ever get it; and so, we teach ourselves to be nonchalant, to shrug our shoulders and accept that what we have as our lot in life is all that we deserve.

The mantra 'It is so amazing to feel the flow of desire and abundance fill every pore of my being' reminds us that at the very core of our being is the joy and the excitement of the experience of living; Living, not just existing day-to-day, but living with intention, with purpose and with desire.

As you say the mantra 'It is so amazing to feel the flow of desire and abundance fill every pore of my being' recognise that to have wants, desires, hope and wishes lies at the very core of what it means to be alive. Feel the excitement in the bubbling of a new dream and the exhilaration of an up-coming journey; recognise the beauty in all of your desires and how they make you more of whom you already are.

Remember, just as the plant turns its face towards the sun in acknowledgement of its powerful aid, so to can you turn towards the waterfalls of all your desires, revelling in the unceasing, never-ending, out-pouring of your worth and deservability.

It is so amazing to feel the flow of desire and abundance fill every pore of my being.

MANTRA 53

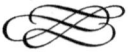

The wondrous feeling of knowing that my dreams and desires know no bounds and that the Universe is constantly conspiring to show me the way.

MANTRA 53: INTRODUCTION

The wondrous feeling of knowing that my dreams and desires know no bounds and that the Universe is constantly conspiring to show me the way.

At any point in time, beyond the reaches and the connections that our logical mind can make and build, there are a multitude of opportunities that present themselves in ways that are often beyond our comprehensible mind.

We refer to these incidents as coincidences; but, are they simply meeting points of accidental fate? Or would we acknowledge that there is a dream-maker who has the power to orchestrate, right in to our laps and embraces, perfectly delivered, uncannily timed opportunities?

As you say the mantra 'The wondrous feeling of knowing that my dreams and desires knows no bounds and that the Universe is constantly conspiring to show me the way' tune in to the vast expanse of possibilities, far beyond those you could think up or even imagine. Acknowledge that with each dream, with each desire, with each want and each longing, comes the opportunity to embrace with wide open arms the journey laid out in fields of possibilities.

Know that it is not for you to command or dictate each minute step to take you along the path of your destiny, but to simply respond to each bid and call that comes to your open heart.

The wondrous feeling of knowing that my dreams and desires knows no bounds and that the Universe is constantly conspiring to show me the way.

MANTRA 54

Wonderful experiences punctuate my life and make me pause to revel in how beautiful life truly is.

MANTRA 54: INTRODUCTION

Wonderful experiences punctuate my life and make me pause to revel in how beautiful life truly is.

The mantra 'Wonderful experiences punctuate my life and make me pause to revel in how beautiful life truly is' helps us to focus on what it means to truly see the best in all facets of our lives.

In the hustle and bustle of every day life, getting children off to school, dashing to the workplace; in our urgency to 'get things done' we are blind to the meeting points of the thousands of things going right in order to carry us on through the day.

From the cooperation of all the cells and muscles in our body, to the 'just right' chemical reactions that need to take place in order start the engine of a vehicle; from the perfect combination of food from which your body derives its energy to the subtle, delicate balance of the perfect environment in which we all live; life takes place in all the little magical moments that we so often overlook.

As you say the mantra 'Wonderful experiences punctuate my life and make me pause to revel in how beautiful life truly is' make a pact with yourself, that today, you will be on the look out for something extraordinary no matter how simple it may seem; the perfect combination of colors in the morning sunrise, or a gorgeous piece of toast at breakfast time; the perfect blend of coffee, the wonderful toothless grin of a baby.

Smile, as you look forward to the million little joys that will fill your day as you begin to look out for them; open your mind and your heart, accepting, welcoming and embracing the wonderful, beautiful life that you already lead everyday.

Wonderful experiences punctuate my life and make me pause to revel in how beautiful life truly is.

MANTRA 55

The ability to desire and manifest is but one of the many human talents I am born with, knowing that with each moment of allowing, a more magical life begins.

MANTRA 55: INTRODUCTION

The ability to desire and manifest is but one of the many human talents I am born with, knowing that with each moment of allowing, a more magical life begins.

The mantra 'The ability to desire and manifest is but one of the many human talents that I am born with, knowing that with each moment of allowing, a more magical life begins' seeks to remind us that this journey we take through life is an adventure in identifying our wants and needs, hopes and dreams.

No matter where we stand on the path through life, each of us would willingly acknowledge that there is always more that we desire, whether material things or progress in spiritual and mental states of being. Learning to accept this innate desire and therefore embrace its path is part of who we are and our life's journey.

As you say the mantra 'The ability to desire and manifest is but one of the many human talents that I am born with, knowing that with each moment of allowing, a more magical life begins' prepare to embrace all aspects yourself and your journey.

Feel the acceptance and the recognition of the paths that will unfold before you. Begin to acknowledge, with joy and contentment, that you are ready, ready to be surprised, ready to be amazed, ready to be carried along the drifts of the currents that you know will guide and bring you to the shores of all of your desires.

The ability to desire and manifest is but one of the many human talents that I am born with, knowing that with each moment of allowing, a more magical life begins.

MANTRA 56

Money desires an environment that is happy and welcoming of it, it does not care about my creed or colour - only that I care and respect myself enough to know that I are worthy of it.

MANTRA 56: INTRODUCTION

Money desires an environment that is happy and welcoming of it, it does not care about my creed or colour - only that I care and respect myself enough to know that I are worthy of it.

The mantra 'Money desires an environment that is happy and welcoming of it, it does not care about my creed or color - only that I care and respect myself enough to know that I am worthy of it' reminds us that although the greatest desires of wealth are created in moments of lack, the flow of money comes not when we are focused on the limits of our abilities and capabilities but only when we are able to open the flood-gates to embrace the abundance that surrounds us and is naturally due to us.

One of the biggest limitations in our journey to wealth is the perception that what we present in exchange for money has to be, in our perspective, worthwhile. Based on our typical working experience, we naturally think in terms of effort and of time in exchange for money, very rarely do we ever consider that there are a variety of sources and a multitude of ways in which riches may come to us.

As you say the mantra 'Money desires an environment that is

happy and welcoming of it, it does not care about my creed or color - only that I care and respect myself enough to know that I am worthy of it' remember the gratitude and appreciation you feel for the wealth that you already have. Feel what joyous fun and great ease it is to exchange the money you have for any of the goods and services that you desire.

As you begin to embrace the unbridled excitement of surprise that corresponds to a steadfast belief in your own self-worth and value, as you open up to the concept of accepting and of allowing, you will find yourself in constant receipt of favors far beyond your imaginings.

Money desires an environment that is happy and welcoming of it, it does not care about my creed or color - only that I care and respect myself enough to know that I am worthy of it.

MANTRA 57

Abundance is the birthright of every person; and so it is, also for me.

MANTRA 57: INTRODUCTION

Abundance is the birthright of every person; and so it is, also for me.

The mantra 'Abundance is the birthright of every person; and so it is, also for me' invites us to embrace a knowing that has long existed; in a time before each of us were capable of defining and of deciding on our limiting logical beliefs.

The all-encompassing notions of birthright, typically force us to define our current positions in relation to an earlier preconceived situation. One in which we have had little control or bearing beyond the circumstances of our birth. We are often demarcated by the society in which we were raised, by the choice of our peers and surroundings and by the happenings and occasions that mark our time.

Rarely are we ever able to reconnect and to transcend the limitless force of nature, of unlimited anticipation, hope and of the potential that envelopes and surrounds the emergence of a new life, our very own.

As you say the mantra 'Abundance is the birthright of every person; and so it is, also for me' remember with a vast, open heart, the unlimited potential, the exciting exuberant promise of fun, journeys and adventures that lay before you as you made your way in to this world.

Feel with joyous abandon, the limitless possibilities of all that you dare to dream and remind yourself that yours is always to be a life of never-ending opportunity, of endless beautiful days and of wondrous ease and luxuries.

Abundance is the birthright of every person; and so it is, also for me.

MANTRA 58

My time here on this Earth is not simply marked by the passing years of life but by all the joyous moments that congregate and spring forth.

MANTRA 58: INTRODUCTION

My time here on this Earth is not simply marked by the passing years of life but by all the joyous moments that congregate and spring forth.

The mantra 'My time here on this Earth is not simply marked by the passing years of life but by all the joyous moments that congregate and spring forth' reminds us that beyond the passing of time, each of our lives are marked by the occasions and events that define and characterize our lives.

As we learn to embrace every part of the journey we are on, we begin to realize that when all is said and done, the ultimate joys in life are not measured by the successes and victories, trophies and cups, medals or awards but by the ecstasies of living in the acknowledgement of all the simple beauties in every day.

As you say the mantra 'My time here on this Earth is not simply marked by the passing years of life but by all the joyous moments that congregate and spring forth' remember that you are who you are because of all of the experiences you have lived through; good and bad, harsh and joyous. Each has made a mark, polished and rubbed you in to the sparkling, shiny individual that you now are.

Decide that your life, as it is right now, deserves every celebration and acknowledgement for whatever path it is that you have travelled, the road that lies ahead, is paved with tiles of joy and happiness and of the knowing that no matter where the road takes you, you will joyously embrace all that it has to give to you.

My time here on this Earth is not simply marked by the passing years of life but by all the joyous moments that congregate and spring forth.

MANTRA 59

To live, to love, to allow... these are the only principles of living that truly matter to me.

MANTRA 59: INTRODUCTION

To live, to love, to allow... these are the only principles of living that truly matter to me.

The mantra 'To live, to love, to allow... these are the only principles of living that truly matter to me' reminds us of the core purpose of our day-to-day living.

It is so easy to be caught up in to-do lists, in the bustle of everyday living, in the focused intent to be some place, to do something; and yet more often than not, with our lives filled to the brim with goals, objectives and targets, we seem to lose sight of what it means to truly live.

The emptiness in living that comes from a state of constant activity and doing, is far more common than we would like to admit. We are so easily lulled in to believing that to 'do' more, is to 'be' more; and that in 'doing', our lives are by extension becoming more purposeful and more useful.

As you repeat the mantra 'To live, to love, to allow... these are the only principles of living that truly matter to me' pause for a moment to let the words settle down within you.

Breathe deeply and for a moment, bring your mind to a calm, quiet place. Let the words 'to live, to love, to allow' wash over and through you and find yourself immersed in the relaxation of letting go, ready to drift along wherever the journey may lead.

Be ever ready to embrace the beauties of each experience of life and prepare to welcome the joyous surprises of everyday knowing that with every moment of allowing, your life continues to be filled with astonishments and awe.

There is beauty and wonder in all that surrounds us; and to live in this state of beautiful acknowledgement and embracing, allows us a glimpse in to the marvel that is our life.

'To live, to love, to allow… these are the only principles of living that truly matter to me'.

MANTRA 60

There is no better time to be, right here, right now, living wholly the life of my dream

MANTRA 60: INTRODUCTION

There is no better time to be, right here, right now, living wholly the life of my dream

The mantra 'There is no better time to be, right here, right now, living wholly the life of my dreams' encourages you to recognise that no matter where you are in your life right now, you are living in the very moment of it.

Standing right where you are, supported by all of your past experiences, ready to launch in to the future – regardless of all the experiences you have lived before, from the most challenging setbacks to the greatest astronomical highs, each, has contributed to making you, you.

And despite of our very human ability to look back, whether in elation or regret, and our typical tendencies to look forwards as far as we can imagine, we always need to return to where we are in this current moment.

As you say the mantra, 'There is no better time to be, right here, right now, living wholly the life of my dreams' feel yourself relax in to the present moment. Relinquish all thoughts of the future, let go of the past and of any expectations that you currently hold.

Bring yourself completely here, right now, in to this present moment and stay for a while. Acknowledge that where you are right now is the exact place that you are meant to be; there is no better time or place for you to be the complete whole of who you are.

There is no better time to be, right here, right now, living wholly the life of my dreams.

ACKNOWLEDGMENTS

Thank you for reading A Year of Money and Abundance. We hope you have enjoyed it and that it has brought and will continue to bring you, a magical year of abundance.

Please do help others discover this book by leaving a review.

Also remember to sign up for your free accompanying PDF workbook and newsletter at www.lilingooi.com/ayma

ABOUT THE AUTHOR

Li-ling Ooi is a doer, a thinker, and a lover of life. She sees so much, in and of this world, to value and appreciate, and has learnt that the gifts that await us, surround and envelop us constantly and immeasurably.

She writes of things that inspire, encourage and uplift her, in hopes of sharing that inspiration with the world at large. She enjoys beautiful walks, curling up with a good book, and time spent with family and friends.

If you have enjoyed reading this book or have any questions, she would love to hear from you. She can be reached on social media or via her website at www.lilingooi.com

ALSO BY LI-LING OOI

COMING SOON:

A YEAR OF LOVE AND LAUGHTER
A YEAR OF HEALTH AND WELL-BEING
THE SECRET CONVERSATIONS
LIVE THE MONEY FLOW

Oxford University Press:
PRINCIPLES OF X-RAY CRYSTALLOGRAPHY

www.ingramcontent.com/pod-product-compliance
Lightning Source LLC
Chambersburg PA
CBHW071438080526
44587CB00014B/1905